PORTRAITS OF

ALABAMA

by Lissa Johnston

Gareth Stevens
Publishing

Please visit our web site at: www.garethstevens.com
For a free color catalog describing Gareth Stevens Publishing's
list of high-quality books and multimedia programs, call
1-800-542-2595 (USA) or 1-800-387-3178 (Canada).
Gareth Stevens Publishing's fax: (877) 542-2596.

Library of Congress Cataloging-in-Publication Data

Johnston, Lissa.
    Alabama / Lissa Johnston.
      p. cm. — (Portraits of the states)
    Includes bibliographical references and index.
    ISBN-10: 0-8368-4659-1   ISBN-13: 978-0-8368-4659-1(lib. bdg.)
    ISBN-10: 0-8368-4678-8   ISBN-13: 978-0-8368-4678-2 (softcover)
    1. Alabama—Juvenile literature. I. Title. II. Series.
  F326.3.J64   2006
  976.1—dc22   2005051744

Updated edition reprinted in 2008. First published in 2006 by
Gareth Stevens Publishing
A Weekly Reader® Company
1 Reader's Digest Rd.
Pleasantville, NY 10570-7000 USA

Copyright © 2006 by Gareth Stevens, Inc.

Editorial direction: Mark J. Sachner
Project manager: Jonatha A. Brown
Editor: Catherine Gardner
Art direction and design: Tammy West
Picture research: Diane Laska-Swanke
Indexer: Walter Kronenberg
Production: Jessica Morris and Robert Kraus

Picture credits: Cover, pp. 6, 15, 20, 24, 25 © John Elk III; pp. 4, 16, 22
© Gibson Stock Photography; p. 5 © Corel; p. 8 © MPI/Getty Images; p. 9
© North Wind Picture Archives; p. 11 © Gabriel Benzur/Time & Life Pictures/
Getty Images; p. 17 © Stock Montage/Getty Images; p. 26 © Grant Halverson/
Getty Images; p. 27 © Ron Sachs/Pool/Getty Images; p. 28 Huntsville Convention
& Visitors Bureau; p. 29 Alabama Bureau of Tourism & Travel/Karim Basha

Printed in the United States of America

3 4 5 6 7 8 9 10 09 08

CONTENTS

Words that are defined in the Glossary appear
in **bold** the first time they are used in the text.

On the Cover: Rocket Park, at the U.S. Space and Rocket Center
in Huntsville.

Introduction

Do you enjoy playing at the beach? Or fishing in rivers? Do you like going to festivals and eating great food? How about visiting old battlegrounds? Or learning to land the space shuttle? You can do all of these things and more in Alabama.

Alabama has so much to see. In the south, ocean waves splash the beach. Mountains rise in the north. Bears, bobcats, and turkeys live in the woods. Turtles and alligators swim in the swamps.

This state has a rich history, and its people are proud of their past. They enjoy having visitors. Alabama is a warm and friendly place to live or visit!

Children ride the Multi-Axis Trainer (MAT) at the U.S. Space & Rocket Center Space Camp, in Huntsville.

The state flag of Alabama.

ALABAMA FACTS

- Became the 22nd U.S. State: December 14, 1819
- Population (2007): 4,627,851
- Capital: Montgomery
- Biggest Cities: Birmingham, Montgomery, Mobile, Huntsville
- Size: 50,744 square miles (131,426 square kilometers)
- Nickname: The Heart of Dixie
- State Tree: Southern longleaf pine
- State Flower: Camellia
- State Insect: Monarch butterfly
- State Bird: Yellowhammer

History

The first groups of Native Americans came to Alabama thousands of years ago. They moved from place to place and lived in caves. They ate plants that grew wild and animals that they hunted. Later, Natives made huts from animal skins. They grew squash and corn. By the 1600s, at least five different groups lived in the area.

Early Explorers

In 1519, Spanish explorer Alonso Alvarez de Piñeda sailed along the coast of Alabama and into Mobile Bay. Forty years later, the Spanish built small towns near the bay. Storms ruined their ships and supplies. The settlers nearly starved. Their towns failed.

Early Native people built these huge mounds of earth. The mounds can still be seen near Tuscaloosa.

Treasure Hunt

Hernando de Soto was a Spanish explorer. He and his men came through Alabama in 1540. They were looking for gold. Angry Natives tried to drive them away. De Soto left the area without finding gold.

Explorers from France did better. They built the first lasting European settlements in Alabama. One settlement was Fort Louis de la Mobile. It was built in 1702. It later became the city of Mobile.

A New Nation

Britain had land in America, too. Its thirteen **colonies** were on the East Coast. Britain, France, and Spain fought over land in America for many years. In 1763, Britain won a war against France. Britain took most of the French land, including Alabama.

The thirteen colonies wanted to be free of British rule. They went to war with Britain in 1775. Spain attacked the British, too. It captured the city of Mobile.

The thirteen colonies won the Revolutionary War in 1783. They formed the United States. This new country then took most of Alabama from Britain, but Spain kept Mobile. In 1813, the U.S. took Mobile too.

Natives and Settlers

More white settlers moved to the area. Many of them were

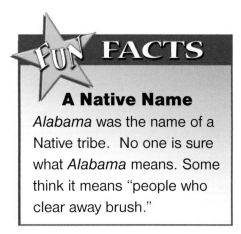

FACTS

A Native Name
Alabama was the name of a Native tribe. No one is sure what *Alabama* means. Some think it means "people who clear away brush."

William Weatherford was also known as Chief Red Eagle. He surrendered to Andrew Jackson after the Battle of Horseshoe Bend.

farmers. They took land from the Natives. Some of the Natives fought to keep their land. One big battle took place at Horseshoe Bend in 1814. The settlers and General Andrew Jackson won. Native attacks ended after this battle.

The Alabama Territory was formed in 1817. Two years later, Alabama became the twenty-second state. Its first capital was Huntsville.

Even more white settlers moved to Alabama. They forced many Natives to leave the state in the 1830s. These Natives were forced to go to what is now Oklahoma.

The Civil War

Some farmers built large farms called **plantations**. African American slaves did most of the work on these plantations.

Slavery was not legal in the Northern states. Many people in the North wanted to end slavery in the South, too. Southern slave owners did not agree. The two sides argued about slavery during the 1850s.

In 1861, Abraham Lincoln became president. People in Alabama did not like him. They thought he would free their slaves.

Alabama broke away from the United States in 1861. Other Southern states left the **Union**, too. Leaders from these states met in the Alabama city of Montgomery. They set up a new country. It was called the Confederate States of America. Montgomery was the first capital.

President Lincoln did not want the country to break apart. He sent troops to the

IN ALABAMA'S HISTORY

The Battle of Mobile Bay

One of the most important battles of the Civil War was fought in Mobile Bay. The Southern troops fired **torpedoes** at Union ships. They sunk one ship, but the Union captured Mobile. They cut off supplies to the Southern troops.

South. The Civil War began. Many battles were fought in Alabama. Thousands of men died in this war.

The North won the war in 1865. Alabama rejoined the nation in 1868. Slavery was now against the law. But many people in Alabama did not want African

A Confederate ship, the *Tennessee*, surrendered to Union ships in the Battle of Mobile Bay.

Blasting Off

Huntsville is the home of the George C. Marshall Space Flight Center. It helped build space shuttles and the International Space Station. The *Saturn V* rocket was designed there. This rocket helped put men on the Moon in the 1960s. Today, the *Saturn V* is at the U.S. Space and Rocket Center, also in Huntsville.

The Early 1900s

By 1900, farming was still the main way of life. The biggest crop was cotton. In 1915, an insect called the boll weevil destroyed the cotton crop. Farmers found other crops to make money. They raised corn, soybeans, and peanuts.

The state made iron and steel, too. In the 1920s, a new port opened at Mobile. It served ships from places around the world.

The **Great Depression** began in 1929. People all over the country lost their jobs. The U.S. government took steps to help. It set up programs to make jobs. One program was the Tennessee Valley Authority (TVA). The TVA began building power plants and dams on the Tennessee River in 1933.

Americans to have rights. In the 1890s, these people made new laws. These laws were called "Jim Crow" laws. The laws kept African Americans from voting. They also kept white and black people apart. Each group had its own schools, parks, and rest rooms. Places for blacks were never as nice as those for whites.

The Tuskegee Airmen flew more than two hundred missions. They never lost a bomber to enemy fire.

The dams made electricity and helped stop flooding.

Equal Rights

In 1954, the U.S. Supreme Court said that separate schools for whites and blacks were unfair. The court said public schools should serve all children. Many people in Alabama did not want white and black children to go to the same schools. They did not obey the court.

African Americans began to stand up for their rights. In 1955, Dr. Martin Luther

The Tuskegee Airmen

During World War II, black soldiers could not fight side by side with whites. They were kept apart. The first African American fighter pilots were trained in 1941 at the Tuskegee Institute. They were called the Tuskegee Airmen. These pilots flew many missions. They earned hundreds of medals. They helped end **segregation**, too. The U.S. armed forces banned this practice in 1948.

King Jr. led a bus **boycott** in Montgomery. Black riders refused to ride city buses until the bus company changed its rules.

Dr. King also led a march in Alabama. He and other **protesters** walked from Selma to Montgomery. They spoke out against laws based on skin color. In 1963, riots broke out in Birmingham. Finally, Congress made laws that gave people of all races the right to vote. They banned segregation, too.

Hurricanes!

Hurricane Ivan hit the coast of Alabama in September 2004. High winds ripped the roofs off buildings. Floods ruined homes and shops. A year later, Hurricane Katrina struck. Waters from the Gulf of Mexico poured into Mobile and Gulf Shores. The water

rose to 11 feet (3.4 meters) deep in some places. Even so, Katrina did not do as much damage in Alabama as it did in Louisiana and Mississippi.

Famous People of Alabama

Rosa Parks

Born: February 4, 1913, Tuskegee, Alabama

Died: October 24, 2005, Detroit, Michigan

Rosa Parks grew up in Alabama with "Jim Crow" laws. There, it was against the law for African Americans to sit in the front seats of a bus if white people wanted to sit there. One day in 1955, Mrs. Parks got on a bus in Montgomery. The back rows were full, so she sat in the front. When a white man got on the bus, she would not leave her seat. This small act led to the Montgomery Bus Boycott. Some people say she started the **Civil Rights** Movement.

1519	Alonso Alvarez de Piñeda of Spain explores Mobile Bay.
1702	The French found Fort Louis de la Mobile (Mobile).
1783	Britain gives up most of Alabama to the United States.
1813	The United States takes control of Mobile.
1817	The Alabama Territory is established.
1819	Alabama becomes the twenty-second U.S. state.
1861–1865	Alabama sides with the South during the Civil War.
1868	Alabama rejoins the United States.
1915	The boll weevil destroys Alabama's cotton crop.
1933	The Tennessee Valley Authority (TVA) begins to help people from Alabama get through the Great Depression.
1955	Rosa Parks refuses to give up her seat on a Montgomery bus.
2004	Hurricane Ivan causes terrible damage along the Gulf Coast. A year later, Hurricane Katrina hits some of the damaged areas again.
2005	Condoleezza Rice, of Birmingham, becomes the first female African American secretary of state.

People

More than four million people live in Alabama. About 55 percent of the people live in or near cities. The state's largest city is Birmingham. Many people still live in the country. Some of these people live in small villages. Most, however, live on farms or on small pieces of land.

Then and Now

Hundreds of years ago, Native Americans were the only people living in Alabama.

Hispanics: In the 2000 U.S. Census, 1.7 percent of the people in Alabama called themselves Latino or Hispanic. Most of them or their relatives came from places where Spanish is spoken. They may come from different racial backgrounds.

The People of Alabama

Total Population 4,599,030

White
71.1%

Native American
0.5%

Asian
0.7%

Other
1.7%

Black or African American
26.0%

Percentages are based on the 2000 Census.

Then, white settlers came. They forced the Natives to leave the area. Today, very few Native Americans live in the state.

In the mid-1800s, many white people in Alabama owned slaves. At that time, almost half of the people in the state were slaves. After the Civil War, many free blacks stayed. They worked on farms as sharecroppers. Sharecroppers worked on

Birmingham was founded in 1813. It became a center for industry. Today, it is the largest city in Alabama.

another person's land and received a part, or share, of the crops. Often, sharecroppers made very little money.

During the 1950s, many African Americans left the state. They moved north in search of better lives. Today, only one person out of four is African American. Most

The Tuskegee Institute was founded in 1881. It was set up to help African Americans get an education and improve their lives. It is now a National Historic Site.

of the people who live in Alabama are white.

Many people moved from Europe to Alabama in the late 1800s. Most came to work in iron mines and steel **mills**. People still move to this state from other countries. But the number of **immigrants** is fairly small.

Education and Religion

The state had few public schools before 1854. That year, Alabama created a public school system. After the Civil War, black children could go to public schools in Alabama. They could not go to the same schools as white boys and girls, however. Black and white students in Alabama did not start going to the same schools until the early 1960s.

Alabama has several colleges and universities. The oldest is the University of Alabama. It was founded in 1831. It has **campuses** in three cities around the state. Tuskegee University opened in 1881 as a school for African Americans. Auburn

Famous People of Alabama

George Washington Carver

Born: About July 1861, near Diamond Grove, Missouri

Died: January 5, 1943, Tuskegee, Alabama

George Washington Carver was born a slave. After the Civil War, he became a free man. He went to college and studied science. In 1897, Carver began working at Tuskegee Institute. He helped farmers in Alabama grow better crops. He showed them how to improve the soil.

He also had new ideas about how the crops could be used. He found more than three hundred new uses for soybeans and peanuts. Thanks to Dr. Carver, peanut butter became popular. Dr. Carver gave his ideas away for free. He received many awards for his work.

is the largest university in the state. It has more than twenty thousand students.

In Alabama, most people are Christian. More than half of the people in the state are Baptists. Many people belong to other Protestant churches. Smaller numbers of Catholics, Jews, Muslims, and Hindus live in this state, too.

The Land

Alabama has many different types of scenery. It has rolling hills and areas of flatter land, called plains. It has beaches and forests. Many rivers flow through this state, too. They drain into the Gulf of Mexico.

Three Regions

Alabama is made up of three main regions. The northern region of the state is hilly. Central and southern Alabama are mostly plains. The southwest is a marshy coastal region.

The Appalachian Mountains lie in the northern part of the state. Lower hills are also found there. Many of the hills are covered with pine trees. Some of the land in this region is flat. Much of the flatter land is used for farming. The Tennessee River Valley is in the north, too. Its river system and dams provide transportation and electricity to nearby cities.

Plains cover most of central and southern Alabama. Part of this flat area is called the Black Belt. It has rich black soil. The soil is good for growing many

ALABAMA

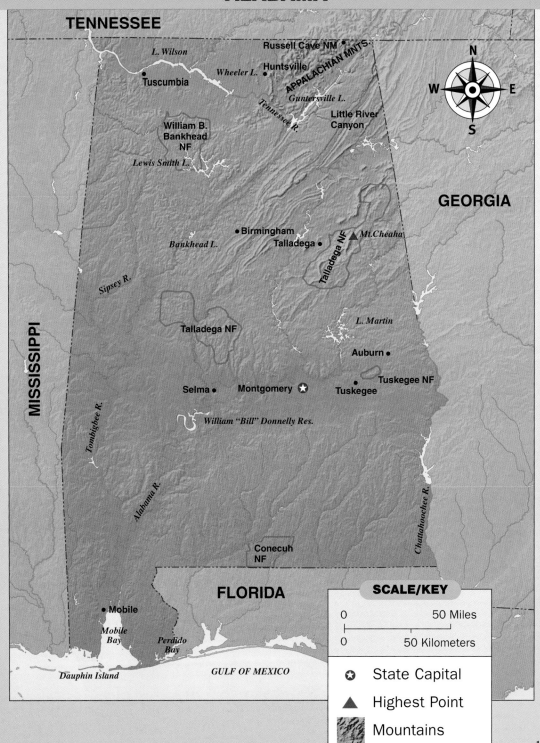

TENNESSEE

MISSISSIPPI

GEORGIA

FLORIDA

L. Wilson

Russell Cave NM

Wheeler L.   Huntsville

APPALACHIAN MNTS.

Tuscumbia

Guntersville L.

Tennessee R.

Little River
Canyon

William B.
Bankhead
NF

Lewis Smith L.

Birmingham

Bankhead L.   Talladega

Talladega NF

Mt.Cheaha

Sipsey R.

L. Martin

Talladega NF

Auburn

Selma   Montgomery

Tuskegee NF

Tuskegee

William "Bill" Donnelly Res.

Tombigbee R.

Alabama R.

Chattahoochee R.

Conecuh
NF

Mobile

Mobile
Bay

Perdido
Bay

Dauphin Island   GULF OF MEXICO

N
W   E
S

SCALE/KEY

0	50 Miles
0	50 Kilometers

⊛ State Capital

▲ Highest Point

Mountains

19

types of crops. Farther east, the land becomes hilly. The highest peak in the state, Mt. Cheaha, is in this area. It rises 2,407 feet (734 m) high. Iron ore is mined in this region. Limestone and marble are found here, too.

In the southwest, the state borders on the Gulf of Mexico. The Gulf Shore is an interesting place. Alligators glide through the swamps. Beavers build dams. Alabama red-bellied turtles climb on top of logs to lie in the sun. Sandy beaches meet the blue water.

Major Rivers

Tennessee River
652 miles (1,049 km) long

Chattahoochee River
436 miles (702 km) long

Alabama River
315 miles (507 km) long

Tourists enjoy visiting here. The port city of Mobile is on the coast, too. The city serves serves ships from around the world.

Rolling Rivers

Alabama has more than 1,350 miles (2,173 km) of

The Little River runs through northeastern Alabama. This waterfall is one of many beautiful sights along the river.

FACTS

Stormy Weather

Sometimes, Alabama has severe weather. Hurricanes blow in from the Gulf of Mexico. They bring high winds, heavy rain, and flooding. Tornadoes are also a danger. The swirling wind of a tornado can destroy everything in its path. Hurricanes and tornadoes can do a great deal of damage.

navigable rivers. This is more than any other state. Rivers have long made this state a good place to live. Long ago, Natives traveled the rivers in canoes. White settlers used the rivers, too. They floated people and goods down the rivers on barges. The steamboat was invented in the 1820s. It could carry many people and large cargoes down,

and back up, the rivers. For many years, people in Alabama shipped cotton and other goods to market by steamboat.

Today, ships and boats still carry cargo on the rivers. Where dams have been built, the rivers also provide electricity.

Climate

Alabama has warm weather much of the year. Winters are short and mild. Very little snow falls in the state. Summers can be hot and humid. Alabama also gets a good deal of rain. The state has a long growing season. Farmers can plant their crops early in the spring. The climate is perfect for growing many types of trees and plants. Hurricanes sometimes hit the state. They are most common in later summer and fall.

Economy

Many people who live in Alabama work in factories. Some make iron and steel products, such as cars. Some build rockets for the U.S. space program. Others make lumber and other products from wood. One product made from wood is paper. Several large paper companies are located in Alabama. The state's railroads, rivers, and roads carry all kinds of goods to markets near and far.

Almost one-third of all workers in Alabama have service jobs. Service jobs are jobs that help other people. Teachers, doctors, and lawyers are service workers. People who work in tourism have service

Cattle are an important farm product in Alabama. They are raised in every county in the state.

jobs, too. They work in hotels, restaurants, parks, museums, and many other places. They help all of the people who visit Alabama each year.

Farming and Mining

Farming is still important in Alabama. At one time, cotton was the only crop some farmers grew. In 1915, the boll weevil destroyed the cotton crop. Farmers began to grow different crops, too. Today, cotton still is the top crop in the state. Even so, farmers also grow peanuts, soybeans, and corn. Some farmers raise livestock, such as cattle and chickens.

The mining business is not as important as it once was. Natural gas and coal are the state's main natural resources, or products that come from the Earth.

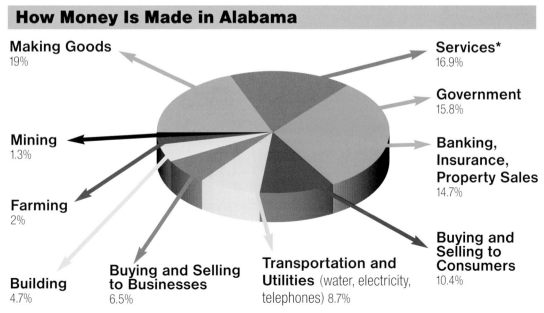

How Money Is Made in Alabama

Making Goods 19%

Mining 1.3%

Farming 2%

Building 4.7%

Buying and Selling to Businesses 6.5%

Transportation and Utilities (water, electricity, telephones) 8.7%

Services* 16.9%

Government 15.8%

Banking, Insurance, Property Sales 14.7%

Buying and Selling to Consumers 10.4%

* Services include jobs in hotels, restaurants, auto repair, medicine, teaching, and entertainment.

Government

The capital of Alabama is Montgomery. The state's leaders work in this city. The state government has three main parts, or branches. They are called the executive, legislative, and judicial branches.

Executive Branch

The executive branch carries out the state's laws. The governor leads this branch. Other **officials** help the governor with this job.

The Alabama State Capitol burned down in 1849. It was rebuilt on the same site.

Legislative Branch

The legislative branch makes state laws. It has two parts. They are the Senate and the House of Representatives.

Judicial Branch

The judicial branch is made up of judges and courts. When someone is accused of committing a crime, judges and courts may decide if the person is guilty.

Local Government

Alabama is divided into sixty-seven counties. Each of these counties is run by a small group of people. A mayor and city council run most cities in the state.

The Alabama House of Representatives meets in this large hall in the state capitol.

ALABAMA'S STATE GOVERNMENT

Executive		Legislative		Judicial	
Office	Length of Term	Body	Length of Term	Court	Length of Term
Governor	4 years	Senate (35 members)	4 years	Supreme (9 justices)	6 years
Lieutenant Governor	4 years	House of Representatives (105 members)	4 years	Appeals (10 judges)	6 years

Things to See and Do

The people of Alabama know how to have a good time. They hold fairs and festivals all year long. Mardi Gras is a lively festival. Music fills the air as parades flow through the streets of Mobile. Fancy floats roll by in bright colors. People on the floats toss beads and candy to the crowds.

The Poarch Band of Creek Indians holds a **powwow** in Atmore each fall. Visitors learn about Native dances and crafts.

Cory Reamer, #13 of the Alabama Crimson Tide, blocks a play by the University of South Carolina.

Condoleezza Rice is the first African American woman to hold the job of U.S. secretary of state.

People in towns all over the state celebrate a festival called Juneteenth. It takes place around June 19. It celebrates the freeing of slaves after the Civil War.

Sports

Football is the most popular sport to watch in the state. One well-known team is the Crimson Tide. It plays for the University of Alabama. Each year, this team plays a big game against the Auburn University Tigers. Thousands of fans come to watch.

27

Many people enjoy stock car racing. One famous racing track is the Talladega Superspeedway. On this track, cars reach speeds of more than 100 miles (161 km) per hour.

Museums and Exhibits

People in Alabama care about the past. Old plantation houses can

Famous People of Alabama

Helen Keller

Born: June 27, 1880, Tuscumbia, Alabama

Died: June 1, 1968, Westport, Connecticut

When Helen Keller was still a toddler, she had a high fever and almost died. She got better, but the fever left her unable to hear or see. Her parents hired Anne Sullivan to teach her. She taught Helen how to spell words with her fingers. Once she knew how to spell with her fingers, she learned quickly. She went to college and wrote a book about her life. She traveled around the world, speaking about ways to help people who could not hear or see.

Students enjoy Space Camp at the U.S. Space and Rocket Center in Huntsville.

be seen around the state. Blakely State Park marks the place where the last battle of the Civil War was fought. The National Voting Rights Museum and Institute in Selma shows the events in the fight for civil rights.

In Huntsville, people visit the U.S. Space and Rocket Center. Visitors see many different kinds of rockets there. They also can try to land a model of the space shuttle.

Outdoor Fun

The state offers plenty to do outdoors, too. Alabama has more than twenty state parks. At the parks, people camp, hike, and explore nature. Lakes, streams, and the Gulf of Mexico offer great fishing spots. People enjoy the warm sun and sand at beaches along the Gulf Shore.

The Talladega Superspeedway is the biggest racetrack of its kind in the world.

boycott — a type of protest in which people refuse to buy a product or service

campuses — the places where a university or college is located

civil rights — basic rights of a citizen, such as the right to vote or go to school

colonies — groups of people living in a new land but being controlled by the place they came from

Great Depression — a time, in the 1930s, when many people lost their jobs and businesses lost money

immigrants — people who come to live in one country from another country

mills — buildings that have machines for making a product such as steel

navigable — deep and wide enough for boats or ships to sail through

officials — people who hold important jobs in an organization, such as a government

plantations — large farms, usually in a warm climate, that grow cotton, tea, or other big crops

powwow — a Native American gathering

protesters — people who meet in public to show they are against something

segregation — keeping groups of people separate

torpedoes — bombs that work underwater

Union — the states that stayed loyal to the federal government during the Civil War; the North

Books

Condoleezza Rice: Being the Best. Gateway Biography (series). Mary Dodson Wade (Lerner)

Creek: Farmers of the Southeast. American Indian Nations (series). T. Boraas (Capstone Press)

George Washington Carver: Peanut Wizard. Smart About Scientists (series). Laura Driscoll (Grosset & Dunlap)

The Montgomery Bus Boycott. Events That Shaped America (series). Sabrina Crewe (Gareth Stevens)

NASCAR. DK Eyewitness Books (series). James Buckley (Dorling Kindersley)

Y is For Yellowhammer. Discover America State by State (series). Carol Crane (Sleeping Bear Press)

Web Sites

Academy of Achievement
www.achievement.org/autodoc/page/par0pro-1

Alabama Department of Archives and History Kid's Page
www.archives.state.al.us/kidspage/kids.html

Alabama.gov: The Official Web Site of the State of Alabama
www.alabama.gov

The World Almanac for Kids Online: Alabama
www.worldalmanacforkids.com/explore/states/alabama.html

INDEX

★ ★